MANPOWER

MANPOWER
Photographs by Sally Soames

Text by Robin Morgan

Designed by David Driver

Introduction by Harold Evans

Published by André Deutsch
in association with Sally Soames

ACKNOWLEDGEMENTS

I have had this book in my mind for many years. It
would not have been possible without the help
and encouragement of many friends and
colleagues:
my picture editor at *The Sunday Times*,
Michael Cranmer; Andrew Neil, Peter Roberts,
Joan Thomas, Edwin Taylor, Hugo Young,
Simon Winchester, Peter Crookston, Chris Smith,
Clive Labovitch, Maurice and Jacky Bennett,
Jane Krivine, June Stanier, Michael Spry who
printed the pictures; Dave Clark, Roger Thomson
and Ray Smith of Times Newspapers' libraries;
André Deutsch; and my brother, Barry Winkleman

Sally Soames

First published in Great Britain in 1987
by André Deutsch,
in association with Sally Soames

Printed in Great Britain
by Butler and Tanner Limited,
Frome, Somerset

ISBN 0-233-98111-X

For my son and for my mother and for E.T.

My friends and colleagues,
past and present of *The Sunday Times*

INTRODUCTION

Sally Soames never quite knows one day to the next whether she will be photographing a ballet dancer or a gorilla. She has for 20 years felt the imperative of the deadline and the elbows of the competition. She has had doors opened for her to photograph the great, and she has had them slammed in her face. She has known something of the fear of imminent death in war reporting. And of course she has known a great deal of the despair of the press photographer. When other news breaks the best work goes in the bin; always it is vulnerable to the appetites of editors and a printing Leviathan blind to tonal nuance.

She has, for all this, never lost an extraordinary quality of wonder. She is forever fascinated by the world and touched by it. In a profession that affects cynicism and is drilled to practise scepticism, she is sensitive and emotional. She has a reverence for talent and virtue, but she thinks well of everyone until they do something irrefutably wicked whereupon she sees Evil writ large. Her feeling for people shines through the portraits in this volume. There are great portraitists, like Richard Avedon, who skin the flesh off the bones of their subjects; there are others, like Arnold Newman, who create out of them a work of geometrical art; and others, like Bill Brandt, who invest the subject with resonances of their own imaginations. All these photographers get to some extent between the subject and the viewer. One is conscious of artifice as well as art.

Sally Soames is always faithful to the subject. There is nothing between us, we feel, and the obsessed, contrary intellect of Enoch Powell, the raw exuberance of Harvey Smith, or the inner torment of Mohamed Heikal newly released from an Egyptian prison cell. The people make an immediate impact on us, but one that is different in every case: compare for a moment Gerald Cavendish Grosvenor and Ron Johnson. But Sally Soames did not achieve these results, could not achieve them, by making herself as neutral as the camera. She felt these pictures. **'There is a certain point'**, she says, **'when the person forgets they are being photographed. You are giving them something and they are giving you something. It is a wonderful feeling — a tremendous closeness of two people. Just for a few moments, then it's over'.** The idea of such an interplay of emotions is anathema to some talented photographers; they fear sentiment may contaminate the purity of the organising eye.

For Sally Soames emotion fires observation; it does not inhibit it. When she visited the fast fading 85-year-old old Lord Attlee she was overcome by the sight of the small figure hunched up on a sofa surrounded by emblems of a life that was almost over. She was conscious of his frailty, but she was instantly aware also of the distracting pattern on the sofa and the dimness of the light and she knew she had to get him to move. She helped him to a desk and he 'sat strong' for just a few seconds then collapsed in her arms. The photograph was never used by *The Sunday Times*; nor was the portrait of Michael Foot taken just before he led the Labour party into the 1983 general election. It was thought to be too revealing.

Sally Soames could not succeed simply as a sentient person. She is accomplished in her craft. She acknowledges her debt to early Snowdon and admires the work of Arnold Newman, Bruce Davidson, Don McCullin, Neil Libbert, Chris Smith and Eve Arnold. Her pictures owe much of their mood to her use of natural light; the portrait of Nureyev was daringly shot by the light of a single blue spotlight she noticed at the back of the stage. And she is cunning in composition. Steve Berkoff's zip runs in the dark like a chest incision, Hardy Amies is framed with urbane symmetry; Edward Heath rises like a dolphin from the silhouette of his black cashmere; the Duke of Westminster, his fastidious Savile Row stripe poised on rough bark, is graced with light; the unemployed Ron Johnson is pinioned in a dark frame of despair.

I first knew Sally Soames as a news photographer. I am credited – actually it was the picture editor's idea – with the notion of sending a woman to photograph Mohamed Ali or Cassius Clay as he was when he fought Henry Cooper in 1966. Ali had never seen a woman photographer before. Sally Soames was a freelance who had been going the rounds of Fleet Street for only a few years following her success winning five guineas in an *Evening Standard* competition for amateurs. She captured Ali's engaging cockiness and not long afterwards, though we did not use the picture properly, we took her on the staff.

This collection of her work is right to be principally of her posed portraits but it is good that some of her news work is included. She brought to it the same zeal and compassionate insight. I think particularly of her picture from Israel's Tel Hashomer hospital during the Yom Kippur War where a soldier from the front communes at the beside of a comrade who has lost an eye. The creative sensitivity that responds so well to people was shattered by the horror. It says something about her that she overcame the fear to an extent that alarmed me as her editor and I recalled her to London. It was in his last despatch before he was killed by a Syrian missile that the brilliant and brave Nicholas Tomalin wrote about Sally: **'Lying on the pebbly Syrian sand this morning, an Israeli military spokesman informed me that I had the honour to be the very first Englishman to be bombed by a Sukoi 20 attack bomber. This is a brand-new exotic Soviet-built aeroplane … But even if my military spokesman was wrong about the uniqueness of my experience, there can be no doubt that Sally Soames is the first English woman photographer to stand bolt upright throughout a Sukoi attack snapping pictures as if she were covering a golf tournament.'**

Sally Soames will not go to war again but she will go on taking pictures on the parapets of life.

Harold Evans
December, 1986

RUDOLPH NUREYEV

July 6, 1978

Four months after his 40th birthday and the
single superstar of dance remains adamant,
powerful and provocative: **'I do not think
of retirement. If I stopped then I know
I would have to be treated in hospital.
I need the dance, the lights, the
excitement. I go on stage now to find
myself, to assert myself, to find my
energy. Now I am in my stride, I am in
overdrive. I am a dancer, perhaps,
I am *the* dancer.'**

CASSIUS CLAY

May 10, 1966

Taken just before his fight with Henry Cooper
and a few weeks before he became a
Muslim, changing his name to Mohammed Ali:
**'The sight of blood really scares me.
Hitting a man while it is still sport is all
right but when it comes to killing him a
Muslim has to stop. Violence can only be
justified by self-defence.'**

ORSON WELLES

February 23, 1967

**'I am satisfied with nothing I have ever
done. I don't think an artist is supposed
to be satisfied. He is supposed to work.'**
The face filled miles of film but one frame
catches a rare glimpse behind the actor's mask.

WILLIAM GOLDING

October 16, 1980

The author of *Lord of The Flies* learned the week the photograph was taken, that his new parable of good and evil, *Rites of Passage*, had won the Booker Prize. **'There never was a writer who did not dream of such an award.'** He has been described as the modern British novelist whose work is most likely to survive. In 1984 he won the Nobel prize for literature.

December 18, 1985

Hollywood cast him as Rambo's Russian
adversary in Vietnam, but in London he is
better known as a radical actor, director and
playwright, an *enfant terrible* of the British
stage and a professional iconoclast. **'I don't
see myself as a genius. I suffer a lot of
theatre. I drag myself along hoping to be
surprised but I am always disappointed. I
wish there was someone like me. If there
was, I would rush out to see their work.'**

SIR MICHAEL TIPPETT

August 21, 1980

On the eve of the premiere of his Triple Concerto. He defines the art of the composer thus: **'To create images of vigour for a decadent period, images of calm for one too violent, images of reconciliation for a world torn by divisions and, in an age of mediocrity and shattered dreams, images of abounding, generous, exuberant beauty'.**

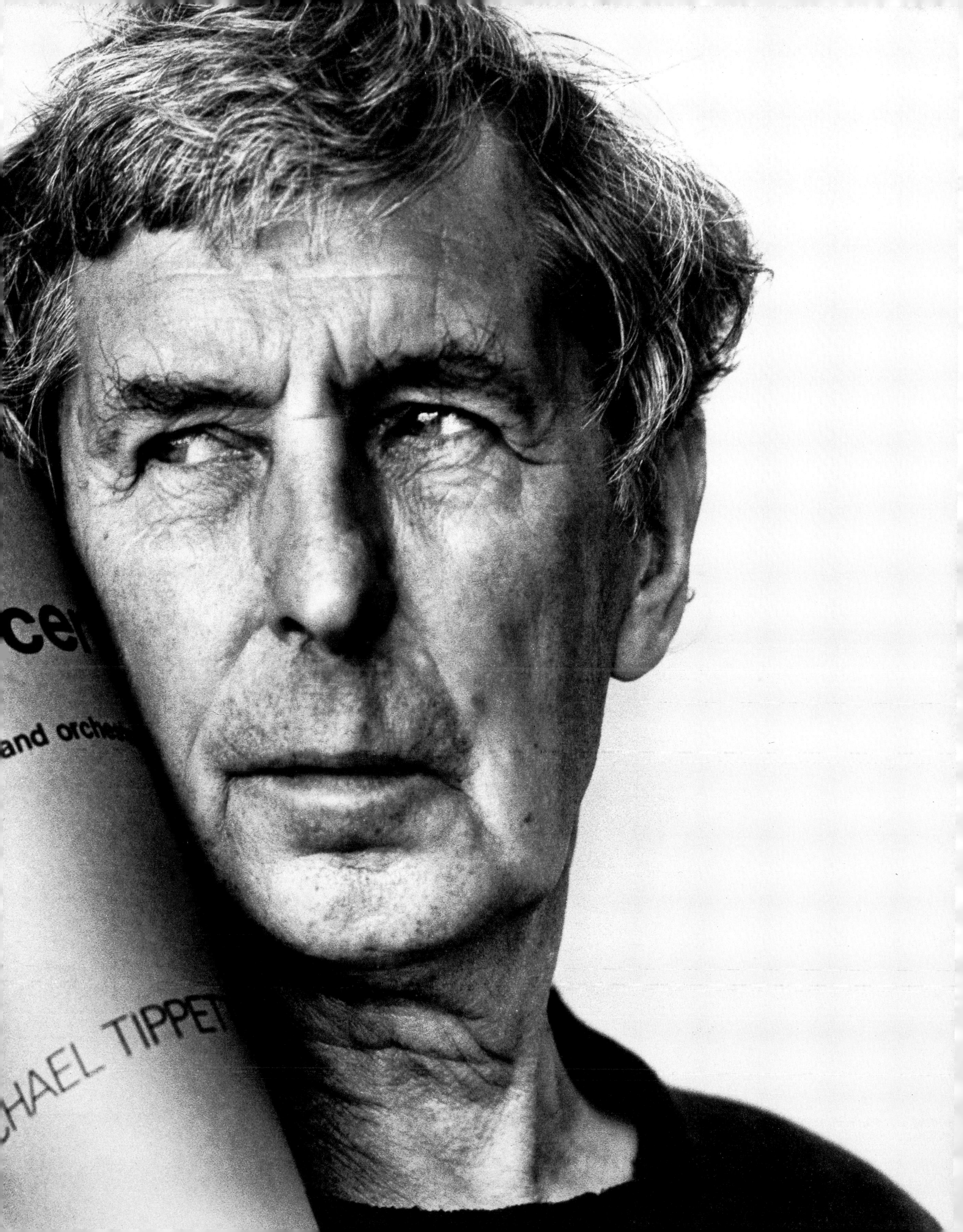

cer
and orche
CHAEL TIPPE

**JOHN
MORTIMER**
September 19, 1985

'It's very important to me to be
English. To me, being English means,
predominantly, having a language that
has been better used than any other
language in the history of mankind,
probably. It means being part of that
liberal tradition which comes from the
19th century, the England of Dickens
and George Eliot and people of good
intentions. It also means being funny —
about everything, never taking anything
seriously…'

IRWIN SHAW

November 9, 1977

Novelist, playwright and screen writer, his first novel, *The Young Lions*, was a title that stuck to him like glue. He was always being labelled the roaring lion of the literary establishment. **'When I was starving they said I was a hell of a good writer. Since I've become popular, the reviews have been lousy.'** When photographed, the lion was sad and reflective.

VICTOR PASMORE

April 9, 1985

He left his job as a clerk with London County
Council in 1937 and became one of Britain's
finest modern artists, **'I wanted to learn
about painting. An artist has to create his
own discipline: he has to find it in his own
temperament. The thing that makes an
original work of art is irrational and
automatic and spontaneous.'**

GIORGIO ARMANI

November 6, 1985

Time magazine wrote: '**Armani has made a huge splash reshaping and restructuring the way people dress – not only the people who wear Armani designs but those who wear the myriad clothes influenced by him. Clothes are the fabric of history, the texture of time and this time belongs to Armani.**'

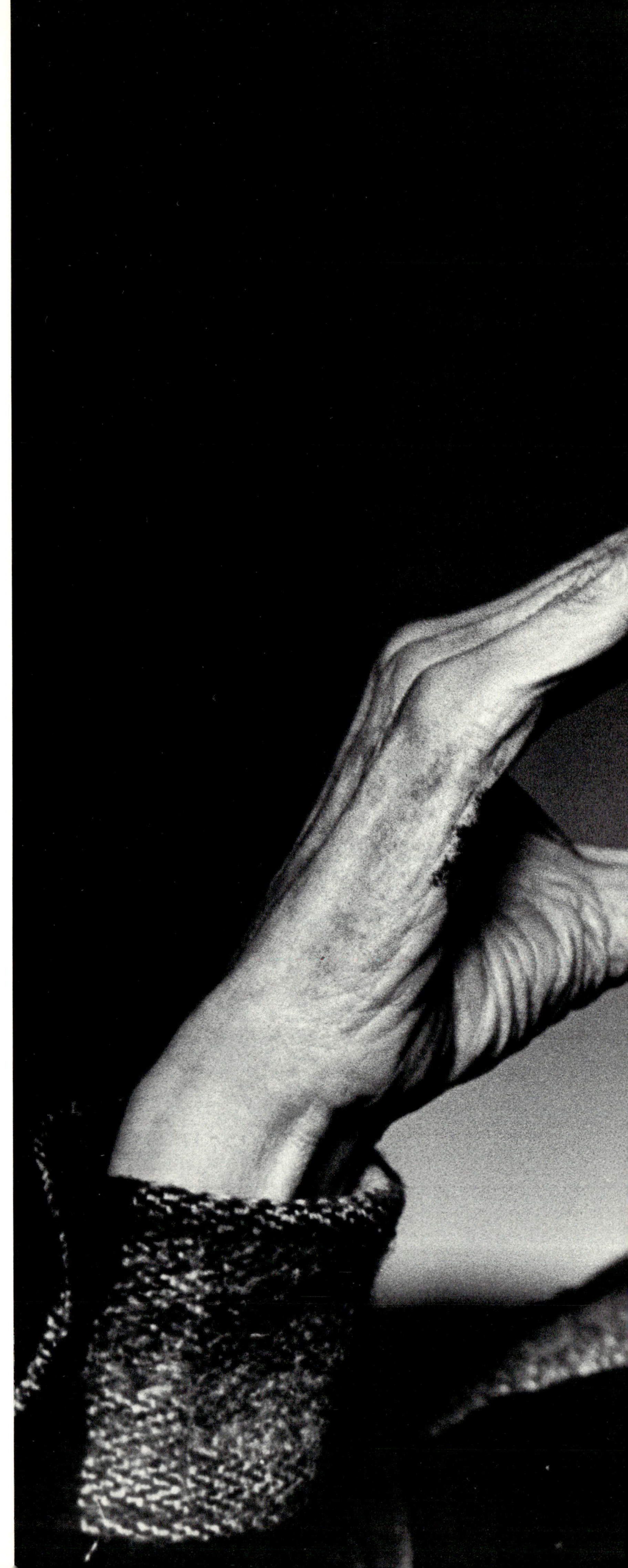

CLAUD COCKBURN

May 19, 1981

Journalist, commentator and communist, he
died seven months later at the age of 77. He
wrote for *The Times, Punch* and *Private Eye*
and submitted his last article a few days
before his death. He wrote the headline that
has since become the standard journalistic
indictment of boring news: A Small
Earthquake In Chile, Not Many Dead.

FREDERICK FORSYTH

August 6, 1982

His books, among them *The Day of the Jackal, The Odessa File, The Dogs of War, The Devil's Alternative* and *The Fourth Protocol* have sold around 40 million copies. **'I've been a pilot in the RAF. Decided I'd had enough and became a reporter, enjoyed that enormously. Went on to become a radio/television man, enjoyed that enormously. Then smashed the whole thing to smithereens by quitting the BBC when I was assistant diplomatic correspondent and going off to freelance in Biafra. Then tried my hand at novel writing'.** He wrote *The Day of the Jackal* in 35 days. **'I told my friends I hoped to make £5,000 out of it. They laughed and said I was arrogant and foolish and that I'd be lucky to make £500.'**

J.P. DONLEAVY

July 9, 1986

The traditional Irish wild man in his youth, he
is now more aptly summed up in a profile in
The Times: **'He is a 60 year old eccentric
who is one of the funniest writers in the
world. He is P.G. Wodehouse with his
trousers off.'**

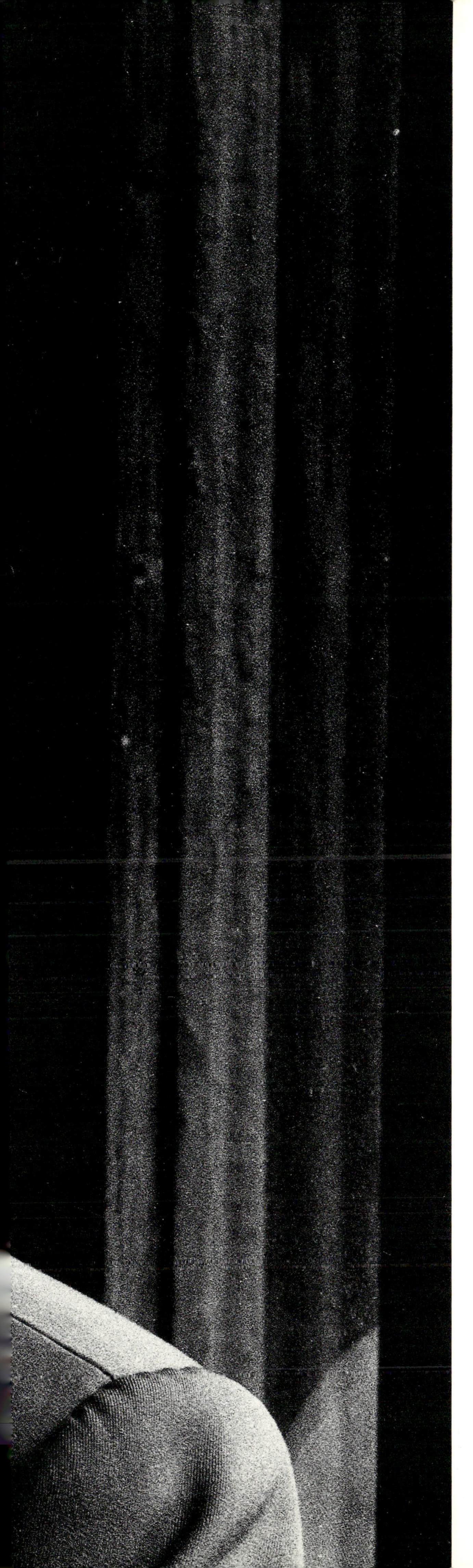

ANDY WARHOL

September, 1970

Photographed at his 'factory' in New York.

ALAN AYCKBOURN

March 10, 1978

Britain's most prolifically successful
playwright, described by one critic as **'an icy
suburban analyst'** is seen here on the set of
Ten Times Table, his directing debut in the
West End. **'Whatever else I am, I am a
fairly good craftsman. If a chap is
walking across the stage, I tend to give
him enough lines to get to the other side.
I tend to pick people who are a lot of
fun to work with. My attitude is that if
rehearsals aren't fun then what the
hell are we doing?'**

SWAN
HOTEL

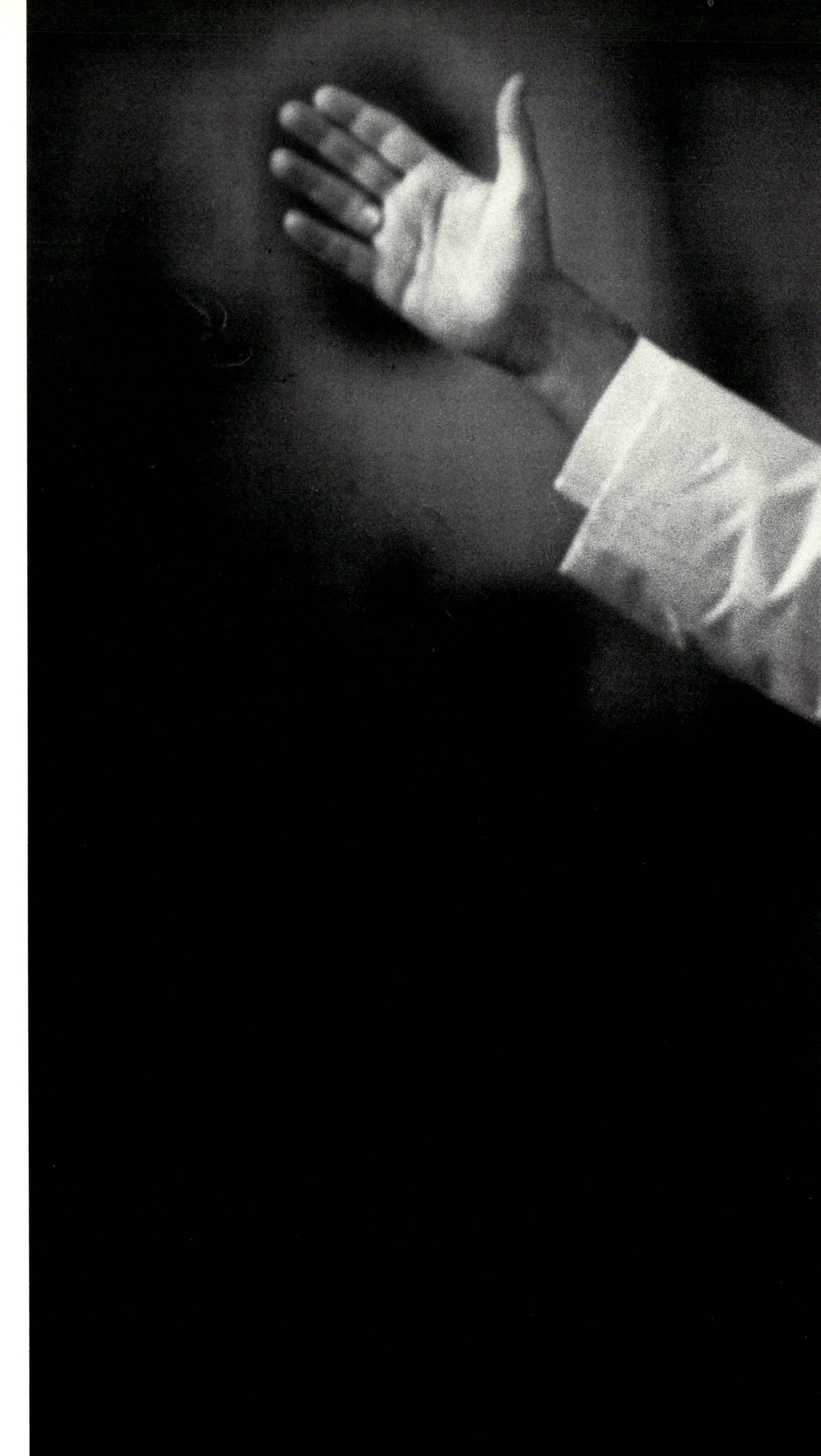

POPE JOHN PAUL II

May 29, 1982

During The Falklands War in which
protestant Britain was pitted against catholic
Argentina, the papal visit to Britain went
ahead. His Holiness filled Wembley Stadium
and portrayed himself as the apostle for
peace. **'I appeal to all the faithful of
Britain…let us give greater emphasis
to the sacrament of penance in our
own lives.'**

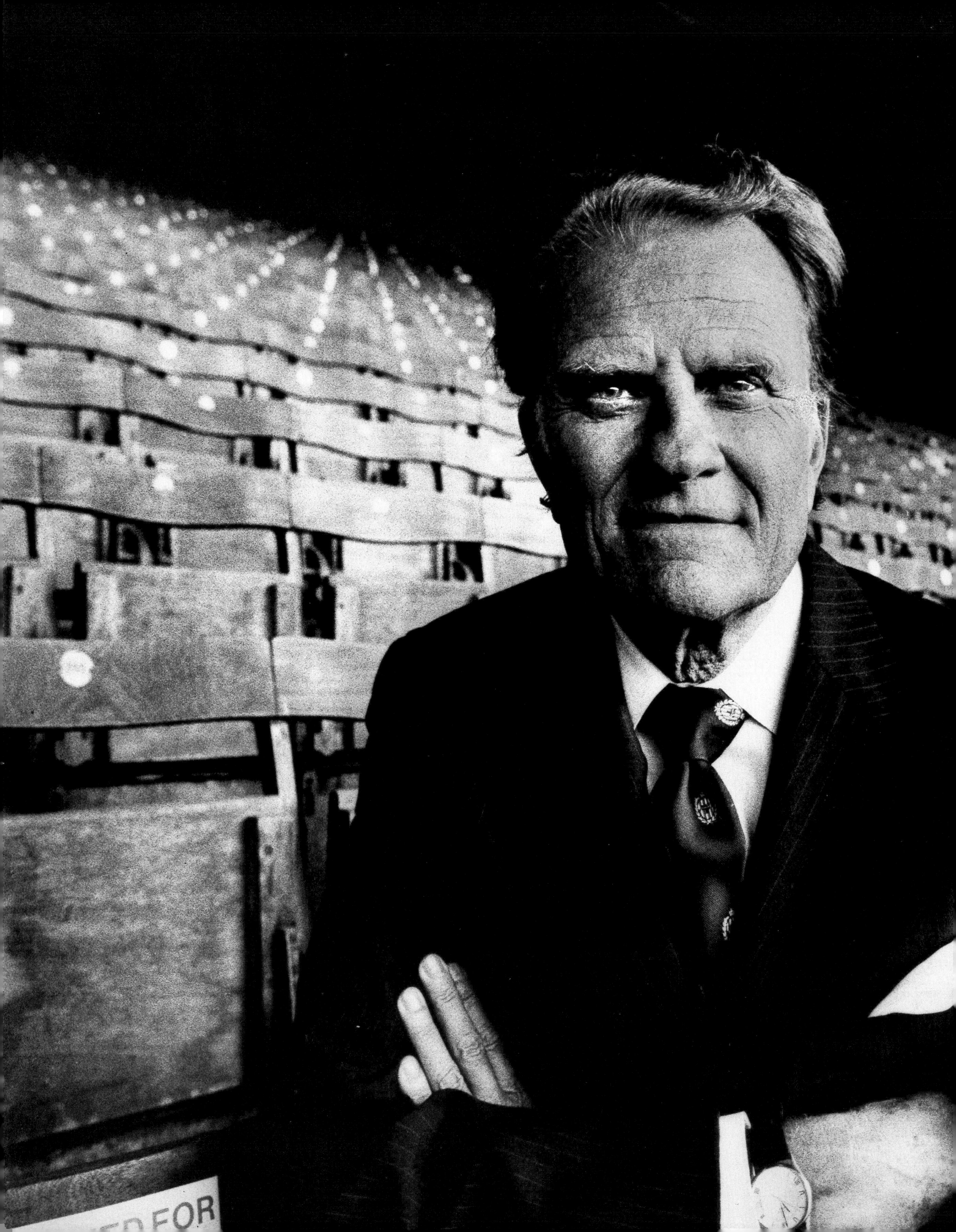

ED FOR

BILLY GRAHAM

July 12, 1984

The extraordinary evangelist is a force
feared and courted by presidents and prime
ministers for a very good reason. He can fill a
football stadium with 31,000 people – as he
did the day this photograph was taken at
Anfield, Liverpool.

LORD ATTLEE
March 18, 1966

Leader of the Labour party and prime minister for six years, Clement Attlee posed for this photograph shortly before his death, in his apartment in the Temple. **'Don't really recognise my party now,'** he said. **'The whole climate of opinion has changed.'** On the Tories under Edward Heath he remarked: **'An old Tory of my time would have said these Conservatives were a lot of damn radicals and socialists.'**

MICHAEL FOOT

March 2, 1983

In the 1983 general election campaign
against Margaret Thatcher, this photograph
was taken at the House of Commons as the
relaxed Labour leader was being interviewed
by *The Sunday Times* political editor Hugo
Young. The portrait was never used, for fear
it might prejudice his standing with the
electorate.

LORD MANNY SHINWELL

September 25, 1984

The elder statesman of the Labour Party
died on May 8, 1986, aged 101. He was a
union organiser before the Great War, served
a prison sentence for allegedly inciting a riot
in 1919 and rose to be a campaigning
cabinet minister and, well into his late 90s, a
power in the House of Lords. Photographed
shortly before his 100th birthday.
A tempestuous and often fractious man,
he enjoyed the affection and respect of all
parties. **'On the whole,'** he said, summing
up his philosophy shortly before his death,
'I like giving rather than taking.'

TONY BENN

February 5, 1980

He has been a formidable voice in British politics for 20 years but never quite acquired the gravitas or the following to seriously challenge for the Labour party leadership. The photograph was taken at the most crucial point in Benn's boat-rocking career: Thatcherism was taking a grip on the nation, the soft centre of Labour was in disarray and Benn was at the head of a left-wing majority on his party's national executive that hoped to take complete control of the opposition and realise his dream of a hard-left Labour party. **'Benn's own chances of ever becoming the party leader now seem scuppered,'** wrote one political correspondent.

EDWARD HEATH

January 25, 1985

Isolated by Margaret Thatcher's ascendancy
over the Conservative party, yet still the statesman.

Arthur's favourite photograph, at Barrow
colliery near Barnsley. On his election to
the presidency of the National Union of
Mineworkers: **'The NUM must never
shirk its responsibilities by continually
negotiating compromises. We must
never fear the employer nor the
government when the interests of our
members are at stake.'**

**ARTHUR SCARGILL
AND KEN LIVINGSTONE**

October, 1984

At the Labour Party conference, midway
through the miners' strike, two men with little
affinity with Neil Kinnock, bend their heads
together during a poorly received speech by
the labour leader. Both have been labelled
**'dangerous among a threatening breed
of politicians and activists'** by more
moderate Socialists. The one on the left has
no doubt he is considered an enemy – his
opponent during the miners' strike, Sir Ian
McGregor, wrote a book entitled *The Enemy
Within*. The man on the right believes himself
a man without enemies. **'I learnt early in life
not to invite hostility.'**

The summer of 1980 saw unemployment
in Britain approaching two million. Ronald
Johnson, 49, was puzzled but hopeful.
**'I learned in May that I was being made
redundant. I don't understand the ins
and outs and it was a bit of a blow but I
expect I'll get something else.'** Six years
on, unemployment reached three and a half million.

CECIL PARKINSON

May 9, 1984

The Tory Party Chairman, tipped as a
successor to Margaret Thatcher, resigned
after his secretary Sarah Keays confirmed
she was expecting their child. One year later,
when this photograph was taken, he
reminisced: **'People I hadn't heard from in
years, wrote to me. Their support was,
perhaps, the most heartening aspect of
the whole experience. I can't recall a
single friend who was not amazingly
loyal. Of course friends are valuable, but
in the end, you are on your own.'**

DR DAVID OWEN
March 23, 1981

Within days of his defection from the
Labour Party to form, with others, the Social
Democratic Party. Owen and his colleagues
promised, 'We will have great influence on
the future of the country, reconciling the
nation and healing divisions between classes.'

'All politicians have vanity. Some wear it more openly than others.'

GEORGE CALLARD

September 14, 1985

Head-keeper of the apes at London Zoo for
47 years.

L.S.L.

FIRE
EXIT

HAROLD EVANS

February 22, 1979

The editor of *The Sunday Times*,
photographed in the composing room
at Grays Inn Road, during the closure
of Times Newspapers.

REG BRADY

November 28, 1979

At a demonstration of solidarity during the year's closure of *The Times* and *The Sunday Times*, union leader Reg Brady of the now defunct NATSOPA, joined hands with his members as others carried a makeshift coffin symbolising the death of Times Newspapers.

NATSOPA

HAROLD EVANS
RUPERT MURDOCH
WILLIAM REES MOGG
January 22, 1981

At a London press conference to announce Murdoch's acquisition of Times Newspapers Limited. *The Sunday Times* editor Harold Evans later wrote in *Good Times, Bad Times*: **'This was Murdoch's day…he was in a fidget…bristling at the questions. I was caught looking foolishly to heaven as Murdoch glowered.'** Evans lent public support to Murdoch even though he had hoped to put together a consortium that would oppose the Australian press magnate's bid.

RUPERT MURDOCH

January 15, 1986

In a newsroom at the high-technology,
£100 million plant he built at Wapping in the
London docklands, to house his four British
newspapers. The photograph was taken two
weeks before the dramatic move.

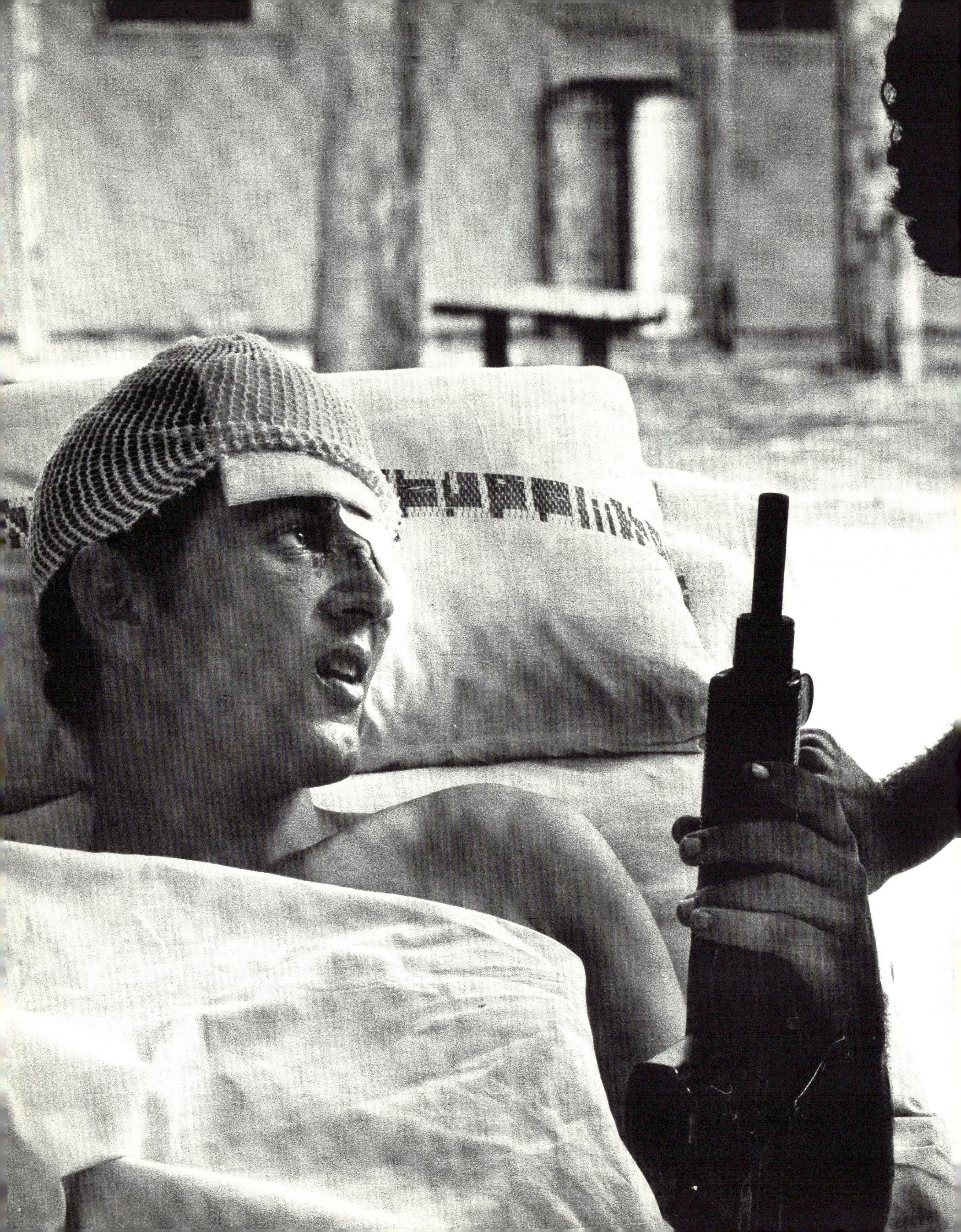

WOUNDED SOLDIER, YOM KIPPUR WAR

October, 1973

MOSHE DAYAN

June 11, 1981

The fighter who dreamed of peace: he joined
the Haganah at 14, lost an eye in a skirmish
at 24 and was made Israeli chief of staff at
41. At 52 he led Israel's armed forces to
victory in the Six Day War but in 1973, as
Minister for Defence, he was blamed for
heavy casualties inflicted in the Yom Kippur
War, when Israel was caught by surprise. In
September 1977 Dayan secretly met an
envoy of President Sadat's and started the
peace progress which led to the Camp
David Summit. He died four months after
this photograph was taken; his obituary in
The Times described Dayan as **'a world-
wide symbol of impish derring-do.'**

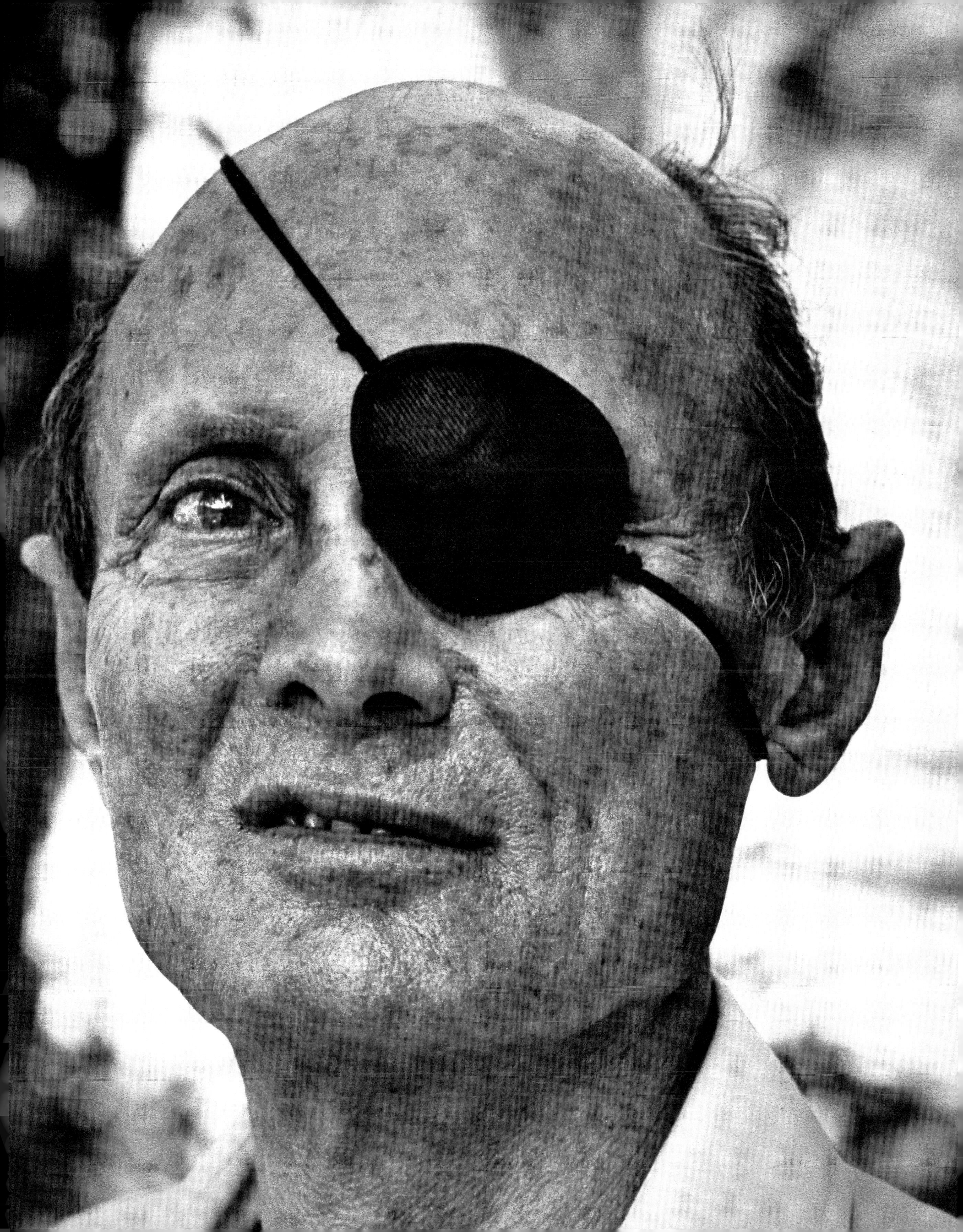

ANWAR SADAT

June 4, 1981

Taken at the Summit with Menachem Begin
at Sharm el Sheikh

'The decision of war and peace in
the area, on the Arab side, is in the
hands of Egypt. On the Israeli side it is
in the hands of Israel. We have pledged
that the 1973 war will be the last.'

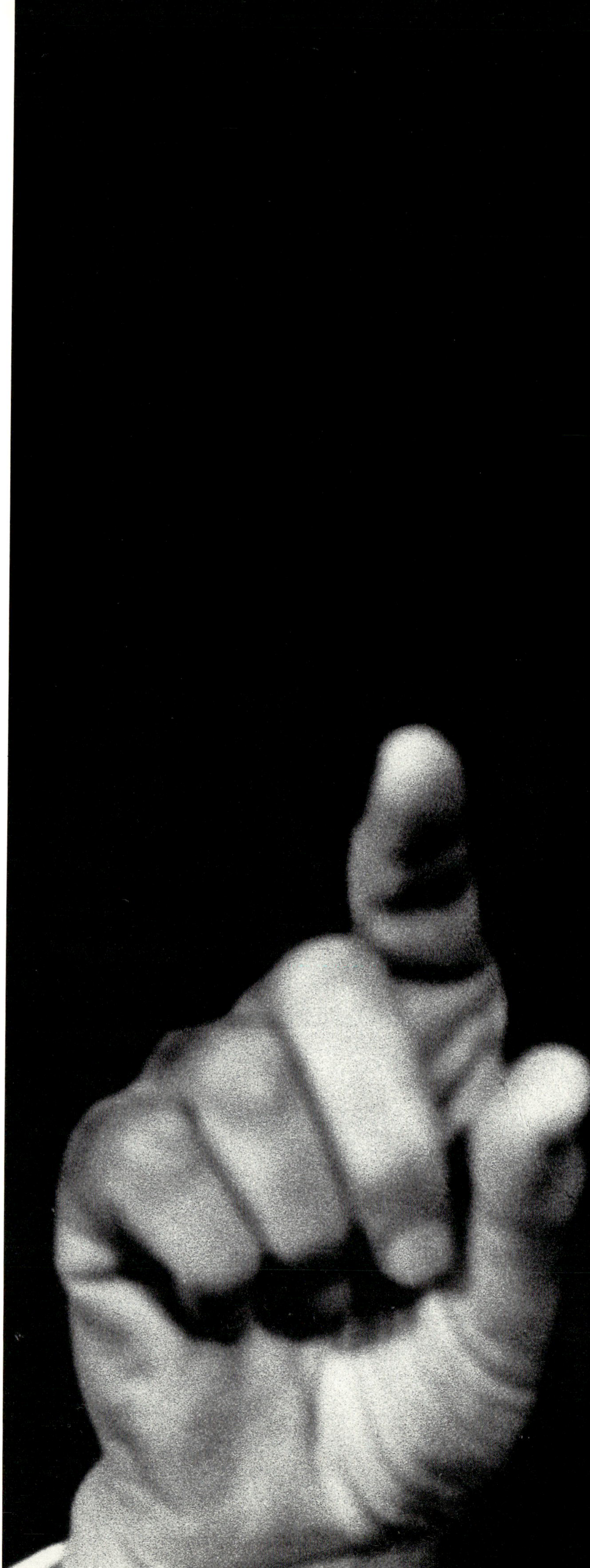

MENACHEM BEGIN

June 8, 1981

Taken at a press conference after he
ordered Israeli bombers to flatten Iraq's
nuclear reactor. Begin believed it was being
used to produce a nuclear weapon. **'Israel
has nothing to apologise for. Never again
will there be another holocaust. We shall
defend our people with all the means at
our disposal. We shall not allow any
enemy to develop weapons of mass
destruction against us.'**

ARIEL SHARON
May 30, 1984

A hero of the Yom Kippur War, the former
Israeli defence minister, demoted to minister
without portfolio after the massacre of
Palestinian refugees in the Lebanon by
Israeli backed militias, was photographed on
the West Bank during an election campaign.
On the hustings he was greeted with shouts
of, **Long live Arik, King of Israel'** and **'Carry
on wiping out the terrorists.'**

SHIMON PERES

June 12, 1981

A man who shaped a nation peers down on another who continues the tradition. Ben Gurion was the founding father of Israel and Peres the young lion whose academic, military and political progress – Harvard, the Haganah and the leader of the Israeli Labour Party – has embraced and influenced every aspect of the emerging nation's economic and wartime survival. There are few national leaders alive today who can match Peres' 40 years of distinguished service to his country. The photograph caught Peres on the eve of yet another apparent triumph. The polls predicted the impending pinnacle of his career, the prime ministership, but Menachem Begin squeezed him out and Peres had to wait until September 1984 before assuming command.

MOHAMED HEIKAL

February 12, 1982

The Muslim world's most respected editor and journalist was jailed by President Sadat on the grounds that he was a '**potential enemy of Egypt.**' Thirty four days later he was freed: Sadat had been assassinated and his successor, President Mubarak, ordered Heikal's release. '**I was in Switzerland with Henry Kissinger. He asked me if I would be okay because we knew Sadat was preparing a crackdown. I told him there was no possibility of my arrest. A fortnight later two security men came for me.**'

SIR FRED PONTIN

October 26, 1967

It seemed natural to photograph him in his own environment – on the beach. But he was caught by an incoming wave as the shutter opened.

HARDY AMIES

November 22, 1966

Celebrating the 21st anniversary of his
couture house and 15 years as Queen
Elizabeth's designer, he remarked: **'The
clothing industry needs the couture just
as the motor industry needs the Rolls
Royce. Without the expensive pilot
models you would not have the cheap cars.'**

RICHARD BRINSLEY
DRAMATIST,
LIVED HERE.
B: 1751.
D: 1816.
SHERIDAN

HARDY AMIES

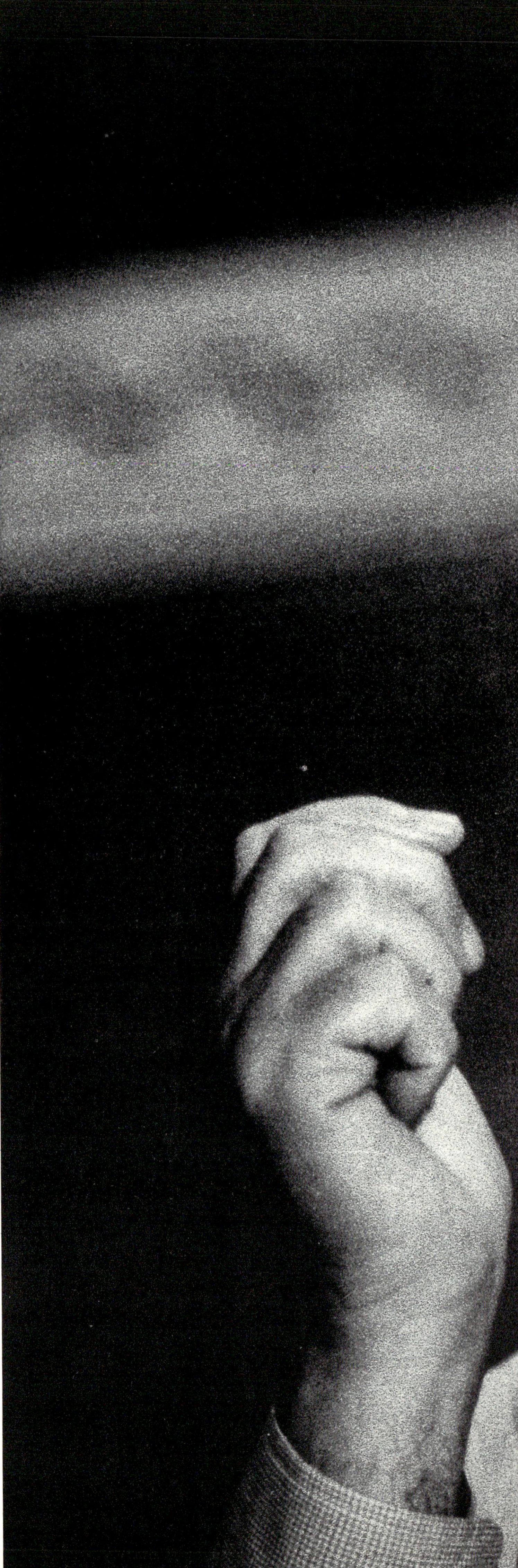

ROBERT MAXWELL

September 30, 1984

'I'm back'. Characteristically ebullient and understandably so. For 20 years, Maxwell fought to become a press baron and a power in Britain. Six weeks before this picture was taken, the former socialist MP turned ruthless capitalist stormed the mighty ramparts of *The Daily Mirror,* put down union insurrection and announced his arrival **'to boost the fight against the Thatcher government.'** Here the subject is in his element – occupying centre stage – at a Labour Party Conference meeting in Blackpool.

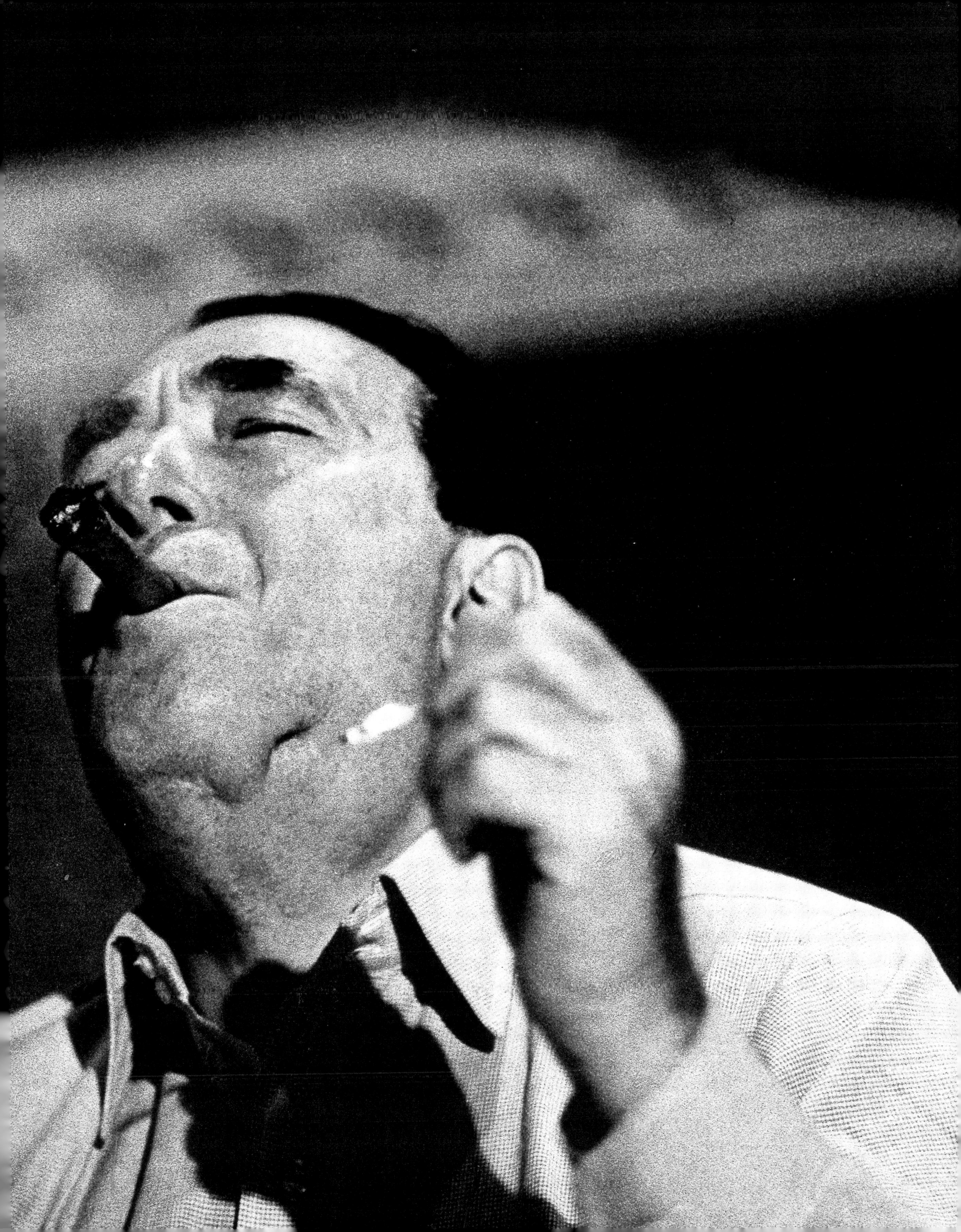

EDDY SHAH

June 13, 1986

After the tempestuous and problematic launch of his new daily newspaper, *Today,* Shah was forced by a cash flow crisis to sell control. In his office at the height of the crisis he continued to present the confident, determined profile the public had grown accustomed to. For one brief moment, however, he dropped his guard when he thought the camera had been put aside. **'In the past 12-14 weeks we've spent so much time fighting fires, we haven't had a chance to sort out how to run a business,'** he confessed.

SIR CLIVE SINCLAIR

October 30, 1984

Electronics genius and entrepreneur.

MICHAEL GRADE
January 3, 1985

On his appointment as Controller of BBC1:
'It's like one of those circus acts where
they spin the plates. You put more and
more plates up all the time and when
one starts to wobble you put another
one up and take that one down. That's
what the job is — fine tuning.'

THE DUKE OF WESTMINSTER

March 2, 1983

The man who owns Mayfair, Gerald
Cavendish Grosvenor, sixth Duke of
Westminster, is burdened with the label of
'Britain's Richest Man'. He is said to be
worth more than £2 billion which earned him
£11,000 an hour at the time the photograph
was taken.

HARVEY SMITH

February 1, 1985

The international showjumper started at 15.
He visited Todmorden Gymkhana with some
friends and watched the competitors
jumping the fences. **'I thought: bugger me
if I can't get a horse to do that.'** The
following year he went back to Todmorden and won.

LORD GOODMAN
June 21, 1986

Latterly the Master of University College, Oxford (he retired at the end of July 1986), Lord Goodman has been described by one observer as the best Mr Fixit in British public life, **'A lawyer to the rich and famous, international negotiator, indefatigable problem-solver, successful academic and avuncular confidant to all from prime ministers to Oxford college porters,'** who once held 19 influential positions in British public life. How did he manage to achieve so much? **'I have the significance in time-expenditure terms, of being a bachelor. I mean, it adds about an additional working day to your day.'**

LORD DENNING

July 8, 1982

The Master of the Rolls had been called to
the Bar 60 years before this photograph was
taken and was Britain's longest serving judge
when he retired. Described by the Lord
Chancellor as, **'a golden legend in his
own lifetime'**. His last words in office were:
**'I wish I could say, as the great man did,
I fought a good fight, I finished the
course, I kept the faith.'**

OLD SQUARE

LORD SCARMAN

January 7, 1986

At the age of 74, after 12 years as a law lord,
12 years as a judge and 25 as a barrister, he
retired. **'The law is a great power in our
lives – a power for good or a power for evil.'**

GARY HART

November 13, 1986

'Running for president is a destructive process. It eats away at your authority and by the time you get there, you are pretty damaged goods. I've been doing it for 15 years. It's been most of my adult life and a weariness sets in. It's a very big country. The challenge to me isn't winning, the challenge is governing.'

M.J. 'DUKE' HUSSEY

October 3, 1986

Appointed the new chairman of the BBC in October 1986, he was chosen by Margaret Thatcher amid increasing accusations of BBC political bias by Tory leaders **'to make it bloody clear that things have got to change, in days, not months.'**

JOHN EVANS
April 20, 1986

Britain's oldest man celebrating his 109th birthday in Swansea.

INDEX